About the author

My name is Chiara. I was born on the left side of the island of Sicily, Italy. I am fully giving myself away through this book. This is me spilt on paper. I am these words, these words are me.

SEASONS

CHIARA DE CILLIS

SEASONS

Vanguard Press

VANGUARD PAPERBACK

A CIP catalogue record for this title is
available from the British Library.

ISBN 978 1 80016 180 1

Vanguard Press is an imprint of
Pegasus Elliot MacKenzie Publishers Ltd.
www.pegasuspublishers.com

First Published in 2021

Vanguard Press
Sheraton House Castle Park
Cambridge England

Printed & Bound in Great Britain

Dedication

To my mom, who doesn't speak English. To
Emy, thank you for being the light of my life.
Grazie per sempre.

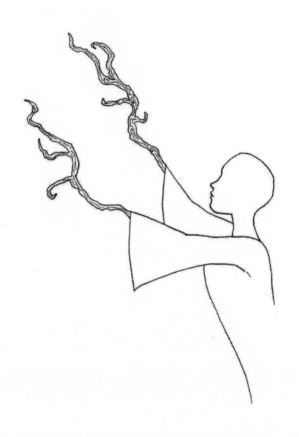

                                    this goes out
                                 to all the angels
                                 who gently took
                                         the gun
                                   from my hands
                           when i was pointing it
                               at my own head

                    —i was a fully-loaded rifle
but you didn't trigger me once

i am sorry

for all the times you saw roses
blossoming on my arms
when poison ivy was growing in me

for my former colours
you were so proud of;
the flowers you shown off
were made of paper

i am sorry

for your silky feathers
and my decaying leather
shivering and trembling,
turning my legs into branches

for all those nights
you cherished the sun in my eyes:
they might be diamonds,
but they do not breathe

light cursed my life
on the last day of summer
which is why
                    i feel
                        the fall
                            inside me

nothing
but the deafening sound
of whispers
to keep me company
nothing
but this mat
made of marble
to muffle the agony

i board on ships
and reach deserted places
i compliment my voices
for overcrowding
lonely streets
and for raising lights
to starless skies

we all rub stones
among themselves
          and on ourselves too
there is so much fire
on this island
so much poison
for little weed
i teach myself how to read
and count the stars one by one
but in this skilful abomination
something indeed is
missing the roll call

          —write say the voices

Shall I tell you of my tears
falling down the steepest slope?
Lilies were forever hanging
as we were holding onto hope

'Give my angels one day more,
give them please one day or two'
when I was begging for some mercy
I wish I knew who to pray to

Shall I lust for the time when
I will lie still all on my own?
Oh those charming charming
flowers,
I want them with me on my bones

The sky knows how much I crave
to tell you how badly I cried
when my prayers were ignored
and all my flowers slowly died

"...as the lovers drifted into self-indulgence and were carried away by their passions, so now they drift forever. The bright, voluptuous sin is now seen as it is – a howling darkness of helpless discomfort."
[Inferno, Second Cycle, Dante Alighieri]

Two rings and seven circles
hold me hostage in the dashing wood
The sap of life is hanging quiet
from the prickly thorny limbs,

and wicked women grow their wings
to overawe me with their claws

these hours
pass so dim and sombre
that i can't help
but feel the tick of time
on my bare skin
in all its lack of entity

these days
follow one another
with the mere intention
of sweeping the square
before the glorious end

this life
is an evil race
and we fall for grace
when all we're awaiting
is a glimmering prize
we don't want to receive

— what's the point of all this rushing
when it is so clear that the sun itself
got sick of rising after the utter dark

it's not hitting rock bottom
that shakes me to the core

      no lights fall on the sidewalk
      and so many times before
      have i licked this pavement clean

what makes my organ spin
and my ribcage break my lungs
is the predictable ship-wreck
at the split-end of the <u>borderline</u>

---▶

what misery
what disgrace
an uneventful beauty
slipped away from my hands
a cascade of tragedies
hit me all over my face

millions of people
were finally looking
beyond themselves

i was dying
to wrap my head
around this planet
but i wouldn't dare
interrupt such blessing

sun and moon
looked after us
from opposite poles
of a lifelong scales

i felt so jealous
for the balance
they had managed to find
while i was always on the brink
of falling off the wire

———e c l i p s e

we are born
with the innate certainty
that your youth
will never tremble
that time
will never knit
your skin in wrinkles
that tears
will never stream
down your familiar face

we'd like to see you
age like wine
but all we get
is a sell-by date

— was your love
supposed to expire?

the same hands that cured my fever
are now lingering around the trigger

i may be the failure
of an artisan
the porcelain vase
flawed at the edges
but just like your freshets
merged into each other
just to put me together
they will now use the same craft
to generate a greater force
and learn its messages by heart

the moon
will make the tide go quiet
just to make them listen
to the smoother silence
of a night portrayed
on the same sky
by the hands
of different stars

only then
will they learn
what peace is
only then will i stop
breaking to pieces

i am but a pleaser.
spot me behind the papers
and my gaze won't be clear to your eyes

i am but a faker.
watch my ashes
when i'm burning down to pieces

i am but a hurter.
please, keep your soul clean
i'm just rolling up my daisy chains

if the birds will fly again
or the waves will meet the sand
this, i do wonder
as i wander wild
through these weeping ways

thousands of hearts in the crowd
thump and beat and batter—
mine stammers, it stutters
while yours is forever still

— the river has just dried out

no dawn in this mad despair
no salt nor sugar to feed us
in this conceited fair of unfairness

i've been busy seeing
the sea withdraw
and the bees lingering
around daisies that grew musty
while the rest of our garden
is irrevocably covered in mould
rather than gold

and no branch of olive
can be handed
for it didn't even
grow at all

no honey will drip
from children's mouths
in these ugly ages

i will engage
in a godless starvation
i will bend my knee
in front of a stairway
leading to empty holes
and heaps of nothingness

a whole ocean
will kick inside a closet
like it's crystal-made
but i will put to sleep
its restlessness
—-and then i'll swallow a flood
i will open the doors
water will drain
out of all of my pores
as if endless tears found
their home on my floor

or perhaps as it's blood
descended from wars
that i myself waged
in the moments of rage
against my own name

and so the same water
my body refused
will become ice
and ice will become
the sharpest of weapons
it will itself assemble
into the tallest of mountains
and i will climb it naked

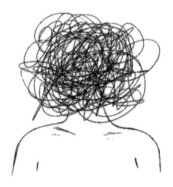

a glacier will meet me
and i'll lock myself inside it
i will fight the fire within me
till the time when it will melt
i will train my eyelids and lips
to rest in peace eternally closed

i won't see
i won't speak
i won't listen
nor i will allow myself to hear
nothing to touch
no fear to face:
forget my face
and so will i.

wagons shifted tracks
and danced in circles
looking for a spot
while in motion

thousands of women
turned off the engines
and abandoned themselves
in an underload of senses
i could merely bare the sight
of those plump bodies
sleeping so pale
under the fiery sun

five twins for each
were morbidly resting
on their sky-kissed breasts
and clouds were smoke
and smoke was air
coming out of their mouths
but they were not aware

that unnatural scene
still replays in my woken head
and little does it matter
if a subconscious worm
made its nest in my chest
i still struggle to forgive myself
for what i could have done
instead of coming undone

i grew more and more astonished
in that crippling lack of consciousness
i had no limbs to move
no legs nor hands to use
i would have stung my fingertips
and weaved silk to keep them sane
but i kept staring at the coma
of a nativity down the lane

—- and i woke up crying

the harrowing loneliness
that holds me captive
when other hearts
beat around me
will never leak out
the damp surface
of the vain words
that are floating
within the walls

—- a thousand crowded rooms
and yet i am so empty

and to think
i had cried with relief
when your voice
walked across wires
and a country
only to nibble my ear
for the first time

ineradicable ink
painted you inside me
as you kept on undressing me
with every word
that casually fell
off your tongue

but never
had i wished nor thought
fate would bring me
to make that call
2.11 in the morning
whispering ever so painfully

i don't think i can breathe anymore
is it the end
is that all
i don't think i can breathe anymore
can you even hear me at all

the holy choirs of this blessed land
cried out low notes
to bring peace in my surroundings
i was longing for doves at my side
but seagulls kept dancing in circles
turning black in a dead-end highway

bishops and nuns sang me to sleep
in the midst of an empty cathedral
and i misspelt my mother's name
in the arms of a red-head woman

slumber wore the dress of fire
and lullabies were dragons
in the hands of fear

— sussex, 2018

england is fading below my gaze
and while my body is in full motion
agony carves me
into plain stone

the grass has lost its green
and all i see is a river of clouds
where i could easily sink in

this railway's too unstable
to carry the heaviness
i host within me

— it has made its home
    in between my lungs
    and it didn't bother
       to ask for permission

reality in-weaves the dress
        and camera flashes and you
        its bright-washed version

      — moonlight is never enough
        to show real emotions

      they will hit you the morning after

END
OF
AUTUMN

i landed on sweetened tears
and my soul is sinking down
in this heavy-watered sea

my golden plastic sorrows
are melting near the fire
yet there is not air nor light
in this land of no tomorrows

WINTER

the black angels came uninvited
among the revellers between the streets.
wolves would lull me to sleep,
oh, how quick the sun did die.
frozen roads made their hearts too cold

flowers and dust led me back to church.
god forsook his promises
kissing goodnight, kidnapping her light

stars dearest, why would you shine so bright?

cherries and peaches didn't taste sweet,
when june stuck them on our tongue
i would swallow them in silence,
but i don't do it any more

one month for each of my fingers,
now my demons live on my bed.
fruit has rotted beneath my skin,
it's time to see the juice pour out.

depression will not catch you
like a beast on an easy prey
it rather will consume you
ever so slowly
you'll almost wish
it could eat you right away

—leave this body
    or serve me on a plate

how can emptiness be
so utterly filling
that pencil tips break
in front of such visible lack

you would undervalue
the space a blank canvas takes up

the very essence of nothing
leads me through a museum of agony
white noise is playing its solo
and we're instruments in her hands

when children's toys drop on the floor
youth doesn't feel quite as before

this saturnine concert
unplugs all the ears
there is no escape
to mask what is here

how do you tell your mother
that you fill your guts with water?
you're drowning in your own waves
and you last felt home a thousand miles away:
they didn't even speak your language

how do you tell your mother
that the man she herself married
makes you want to dive and die?
that your legs are a battleground
and knives fight on them while she's sleeping?

how do you verbally transmit
the way you rub salt and twist the knife?
she doesn't know what happens on your thighs
and so how do you tell your mother
that the room you lock yourself behind
is gloomier than what's on your mind?

how do you tell your mother
that you want to sleep forever,
until your breathing stops and your body's still?

that you, the daughter she so much craved,
regret being born every day:

she carried me for nine months

how do you tell your mother
that the creature she so carefully crafted
doesn't want to belong in the world she put you in?

how do you put together
that the brain she took care of
could burn you down with all these thoughts?
that you feel so guilty each time you speak
you've decided not to say another word?

how do you tell your mother
that school's not as okay as you say?
you panicked in front of your whole class
and what exactly do you do
when the girl who's like a sister in her eyes
kissed your mouth more than just one time?

how do you tell your mother
that the body who's grown in her womb
doesn't want to be fed at all?
that you've got friends inside your head
and you sometimes talk by yourself?

how do you tell your mother
that yes, you do love her,
but please, you don't want to talk, oh please.

how do you tell your mother
that this poem could never end
without making her heart sink in the sand?

how can you possibly
do something like that?

phantoms are prowling again
across the graveyard that is my brain

my apologies to books and blood,
i didn't want you to lie in that box;
my apologies to my bold youth:
you'll be soon be made of wax

as the voices scream so loud
i wish i could somehow shout back
but my mouth doesn't know what to say,
and my words have been taken away

— depression makes you forget your name
     and then blames you for the theft
          of the stars above your head

this loud silence
is made of the crumbs
we refuse to sweep
from our left-over dinner.
adding seats to
this dim-lighted kitchen
will never make us able
to wipe its presence
off the table.
it will keep rusting
the core of this household.
reminding us day by day
that not being alone is a state
that does not erase
how lonely we truly are

i sew curtains
that could shadow
half of the earth

i hang them
'til i lose grip
on what is left
of the living world

i crawl back
to my mother's womb
and attend this dismal show
as it so drearily goes on

— in this life
   i am but a spectator
      who regrets buying her ticket

i wish my words could truly express
how does it feel to be so depressed
if so i could tell you how my hopes melt
all of the times i am dragged into bed
and how harshly i hate each part of myself
when the river where i was baptised
overflows with the tears that you every day cry

i know the ache that creeps in your spine
when you see your daughter coming to nothing:
i feel the same inside my own mind,
the guilt made its home in my brain
and it'll do nothing but laugh and stay
no matter how bad i beg to escape.
it will reproduce over and over
making love with my very shadows
and i drown even when the water is shallow

the walls i built no longer protect me,
i limp my way to the gloomy rooms
and i sell my soul to those who revel
in seeing my body searching wood for a coffin
and watching my soul unstoppably perish

what do you know about the voices so selfish
twisting my arm into signing my sentence
with the blood that flowed on the floor in december

so how could you reckon that it is my choice
to feel as if i am buried alive

charged of the deaths that i witnessed in life
and perceiving my breath as it slowly decides
to get out of my loins and just watch me die

but you'll never think of the hours i spend
counting the days till i'll be made of sand
visualising my tissues as food of the earth:
no wonder you say i don't eat enough,
this illness itself eats my guts alive
i do nothing but wait for the stars to collide
and save from the nightmare
where i keep asking why
can't i awake instead of baring the sight
of both of you mourning at my endless wake
while i weep and weep inside a cold grave

my sweet cries on sundays
could fill a pool in the summer

my gaze stares at the ceiling
as polaroids unstoppably fade
and our rose keeps withering down

when the world gently dies,
the darkness erases my pain
eating my skin alive
and burning my whole mind

— swallowing the numbness,
never have i felt more breathless

the quiet after the storm
never seems to come

the wind is bawling,
hopelessly and forever.
the sky is weeping,
mourning, sobbing.

tears reach my eyes
and refuse to fall.

as the thunder peals,
the complaint of criminals is endless:
my peace is on its deathbed

— the lightning strikes straight to my soul,
waging war and winning the battles

the sap of moonlight barely seeped
through the shut down shutters
of my four-walled oasis;
i so well remember
how i embraced the obnoxious energy
that was meanly shoving my bones
into an aimless pilgrimage ;
so i crawled my way
around the furniture
that witnessed my youth:
never had my room
looked more like a dungeon

— when insomnia grips me into its fists,
        i am six feet under

if mother nature gave me the skills
i could easily picture my wrecked body
thanking the dear universe
for the magical infinity of numbers

and if they ever reached their end
i'm sure in those gloomy times
i'd invent one just for myself

— i counted and counted
but the goddess of slumber
never took me
$\infty + 1$

[insomnia II]

the quiet nights unravel themselves
in the invisible spectrum of time

they so firmly watch me quiver
as i hopelessly
shrink and shiver
and feel the darkness
hold my hands
almost waiting for a friend
to show up and wish goodnight

and the demons do come up
just to leave me warm and wheezy;
my body just goes numb
while i beg for some gracious company

oblivious dreams
hit me back as noxious nightmares

how concrete they are,
kissing my crying cheeks
how unbearable it feels,
as i weep and wail
mumbling tongue-tied prayers
to the ever so distant sun

ropes rape my arms and legs,
and how soon do they surrender
how soon, how soon, how soon

— building walls around the spell of rationality,
i made my home in the kingdom of weakness

the therapist bred the most gentle of smiles
and what about your dad
she asked ever so kindly

it was a bomb dropped in a jewellery

i remember apologising
for all i was able to carve into a sentence
were tears and not words
nothing but a liquid response
that would soon be washed
in a session or some more.
i didn't even get the chance
to mourn in my muffled silence
that she waved it down
with a shaking hand
in that aseptic white-walled space
you couldn't have said it better
went her voice
as a pat on my shoulder

—but i just wouldn't stop sobbing
i just wouldn't stop sobbing

you fear your arms
are not big enough to hold me

would you be surprised
if i told you they are
so massive
that my limbs still hurt
from the heaviness
of your love?

— as you hug me tight
you don't even bother
to see that i'm choking

every now and then
i wear your skin
and clench my fists
to feel the same thrill
you must have felt
when you beat me up
to break me down

and all of a sudden
the years i've spent
under your heavy wings
can still be counted
on my two palms

would you be sad
if i said in front of your face
that as hard as i try to replace
those days
with candid visions
i can't help but hearing in my brain
the deafening echo of a violin
that will never play again?

your voice is graven inside my veins

— maybe it's time for you to accept
    that no sound will come out of this chest
        for you have already broken my wings
           and the bow you bought is scratching

my skin

i used my scalp
as expensive canvas
i painted on it
over and over
to feel the thrill
of a newborn emotion

i would blend the colours
with raging violence
just to fulfil the crazy need
of giving rebirth to
my late sense of self

dyeing and dying
kept drawing
each other's shades
and when my head
was made of stained regrets
  i cut off
    all of my hair

— no matter what happens
   above my brain
      it's what's inside it
         that makes me afraid

when poison's in my lungs,
and stones are stuck inside my mouth
i choose pain over chronic emptiness
i pick blood over water
i pick blood on my body

never will i ever get my redemption
tied to the times when
i used to dance on tiptoes
— and now that i can touch the shelf
sangria turned into cheap champagne
how i crave red cherries on my tongue

when they leave the house
all for myself
i get lost in the path
of immoral redemption

i stare at the walls
'til i put them to shame
in an invisible corner
you should see the way
they break themselves down

brick
by brick
by brick

a work of a lifetime
coming to ruin
in the middle
of a miserable rubble
where i stand aloof
planning my downfall

—- the most painful of baptisms
happened in my own home

                    so i did something i shouldn't have
                    done
i did it at home behind my own back
eyelids infected and band-aids on tears
slaughtered myself and ate me for dinner

so i did something i shouldn't have done
i did it at school 'cause i couldn't breathe
asked for permission to go unlock my lungs
should have been counting numbers,

                            yet i count on my numbness

so i did something something i shouldn't have done
in toilets in bars off planes and on cars
for guilt and for pleasure, for the blind sight of pain
i crucified my time in vain and i even skipped my
lesson

i cried forgive me to the stars
i still don't know what i have done

my loveless nurse

i often feel you under my skin

you touch my strings,
you rive them all
and broken violins play my death march

but when i rise with the dear sun
i kiss my scars and mend my soul
— so watch these choirs
sing me a hymn
as we wait for the moon to come

...and all at once
a lightning hit me
as a tragic epiphany

how will fresh air
ever come in
if i only open the windows
to shower myself
in boiling waters?

— the nightingales paused their song
        to come and whisper to my ears;
                        i never heard from them again

BEGINNING
OF SPRING

the immortal remembrance
of a nurturing torture
still tickles my animal instinct

a chain of two hundred days
keeping me fasting
and forever deprived
in the void go to a wilderness
in which i'd carved myself inside

and i swear on this very skin
that in front of such longevous pain
the wood of long-lived tress
would lose its mighty green

and she who first saw me naked
got hit by the heaviest rock
she daily sated these pockets
so that i'd satiate my body
and how meanly i responded
to such selflessness
and care

but today, dear, must i say
you could make an iceberg melt
and the tallest mountain move
it has never been on you
if i slenderised myself
and refused your soothing sugar
to sprinkle salt on this wicked mess

but i hope
one day you'll see
that all of this
was greater than me
and each gramme of attention
weighed a little bit too much
and weakness erased gratitude
and food had me for lunch

— to my mom.
our world fell upside down
we owe each other no apology
maybe just one to ourselves

wind and water
rescued my rebellious brain
from the risks of the river
that streamed down your eyes

i stare at my thighs
where my past lies
and despite the despise
you'd still be surprised
to experience the sorrow
of saying goodbye

it is fading to red
and pink
and white
and i find myself
holding onto a pillow
longing for blades
as sharp as that winter

the urges take over my brain
and my muses scream
that art comes from pain
and pain is struggling
to free itself
through the wounds
that once fed it
and i hear myself cry

so let it

let it atone for my ancestral sin
that i don't even recall to commit
yet i feel
like i should pay
for the frozen blood
inside my veins

we've shared our roof and blood
ever since i can remember
―― i guess it's true
when they say my heart is tender
i've been alive for sixteen years
and still i'm moved to blinding tears
when we blow dust off all the shelves
and forgive each other
through ourselves

i wonder if you're aware
that at the end of the midnight wars
poets like to write their lines
about souls just like yours

light-hearted smiles
under a foreign sky
never made the stars align

i wonder if she ever misses
me
as she dreams of white pale shores
and never given kisses

—- our souls met
but our mouths did not

whenever an itch
cries out to be scratched
i wish for your voice
to tickle me
like feathers down my spine
or a kiss upon the lips

—- your words
caressed me more
than your hands
could ever find
the nerve to

the thought of you not wanting me
keeps me up all night
more than the eventuality
of you rejecting my name

and love,

the idea of your despising me
hurts me not as much
as the casual possibility
of my scent fading from your memory

Father

I know the seeds from which you blossomed
I know what's hidden behind your soul,
for I come from the same fruitless tree.

I met the oak that cut off your roots
and they hadn't even begun to shoot

Oh, Father
Fifty springs without a flower
I befriended your barren heart
because I so well knew the one before you.

Blood was lying on the grass,
but was the gun just in your hands?

Father, you who run through my veins

When the rood feels heavy on my shoulders
and our life is an endless funeral,
you let your tears water the garden
and never ask to share the burden

I know the bodies hidden beneath your ground,
for I come from the same deadly shrine—
—and my pain is also yours
and your pain is also mine—

when love strikes you
as the daunting challenge
of two hands
grasping the thinnest sheet
maybe it's time
that you just let go

— paper doesn't break
as hearts do

you didn't show me the way
to the spring of my mistakes
you didn't let my blot sink in
in the stream of a floating rill
you didn't sit by my shore and side
when my peace was threatened
by a wavering tide
—- you barely managed
to take off your clothes —-
as you scrubbed your rusting dirt
in the same creek you then drank up

at last you dared
to even suggest
i should warm up the waters
for the following guests

—i was bone-dry
sunbaked on the course
that used to run
in cyclic motion

don't you dare complain
if i've found the strength to say
you're never welcome here again

you were probably drowning
in an ocean of unhappiness
while i was too busy swimming
in my own lake of sufferings

—- nothing makes me
    as selfless as love
        and as selfish as life

i remind them of my mother.
ever since i first saw light
nothing different touched my ears

yet it shouldn't be groundbreaking
to stare at your reflection
and recognising through that action
the man who sprinkled pollen
on your unshaped construction

walking barefoot
in revealing waters
i know our fears
are tied so tight
they keep biting
each other's tail

but what comes across as wrath
hides more than we can fathom:
we dread the chance
of mirroring our soul
'cause we'd strain to recognise
what we think we are made of

—-we share more than we believe
     in the end, we come from the same tree

why do we keep forgetting this

undreds of years from today
new earthlings will be here to stay
i like to think they'll think we're crazy
as they cross borders to plant the daisies

they must have been so insane
having the nerve to cause all this pain

you gave away the keys to your heart
though all they wanted was your brain
you wrapped a ribbon around your smile
then granted it to those
who wished to see it gone
you even took all your clothes off
revealed your skin as a precious gift
and what the silly-minded did
was hand you blankets of shame and guilt

they stole artwork from a
museum
but they didn't even deserve
to see you colour
outside their lines

(it never was your fault)

when i was too ill and scarred
i cursed windows with blindness
and covered them all up
with blackout curtains
and shame as rain

now i let the sunlight in.
i am in full bloom.
rainbows spark up on my nudity
and water droplets quench an empire

galaxies soak me up
in a house of mirrors
but my smile is never dry
lands are pregnant with lust
and i'm the mistress
of my garden.

i've seen people
in my own mirrors
come and go like seasons

and just like summer
soaks up the heat of spring,
each one of my monsters
digested a part of my being

winter absorbed the golden leaves
to the point where they
saw themselves so blurred
in the naked waves
of a lonely lake

and when i even doubted
that the cold-hearted
storm would ever end
poetry unveiled herself in my hands
and became my dearest lover
and my closest friend

— these lines are so cathartic
i almost worship their magnificence

we often lapse in the presumption
to act as if we're something other
than mystic frequencies in thermic waters

humans don't
disturb the atoms
and ask them please
to pause their motion
so why do we put
our life on hold
when we are built
off the same vibrations?

—- mother earth.
we are all plumes in your hands

and your fruit is plump and plenty

SUMMER

my dearest darling,

i've been lingering in outer space
killing time and a piece of me
up to the point where i found peace
in the dancing stars around my planet

the most majestic message
unravelled itself
in front of my figure
and it felt like endless orbits
floating around in the garden of eden

constellations themselves
shifted position
invented a language
to put my oblivion
in a long-lasting quiet

> the universe needs you to be okay
> the universe needs to find its way
> to replace the loathing in your veins
> with the pure magic from which you came

so when self-doubt
lingers around for too long
and you find it hard
to trust your own words
hold onto the same galaxies

that fed you with truth

and moonlight and stardust
for your whole youth

—- nature unties every thread

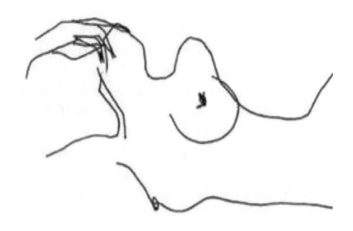

ode to guiltiness and pleasure
on the mouth of first sinners,
long live the time of leisure
when the bride lost all her lilies

ode to mermaids on white sands
and healing weeds in both their forests,
may the milk from the cascade
cure the illness of the sorest

praise the time when
her marks and scars were
softly kissed by the vibrant stars

blessed be the instant
that will not wither
when the rose will decide to leave her

as those around you open their mouths
your soul is so kind and gracious
to grow thrilled by the warming evidence
of their gaze flared up from passion

keep working on your magic
we need more of that

i used to hide
in the countryside
of my home town

little did i know
that a war could
be ignited
by the mere act of love

your deepest fear
is alive and breathing
but your snide remarks
fall on deaf ears

you're not invited at this feast
and the procession i am heading
just won't come your way

girls are on my carriage
there are flowers in abundance

i think you'll understand
that here there is no room
for the bloody thorns
you want to throw

i am almost sorry
your streets are sadly narrow
and the waters of your spring
have never been so shallow

— the greatest act of self love
    was allowing myself
        the freedom of love itself

women
see more blood than they deserve
shattering the ceiling
made our arms all black and blue
shouting up our rights
almost took our voice away
but when they teach us to obey
how can we forget our fights?

we're the daughters of the dawn,
we rise up and wipe the tears
for we need our very eyes
to spot and heal each other's scars

now watch this maze of thorns
grow back as a rose-field
hunted for centuries by fiends
that are now turning to ashes

all your 'once you have a husband…'s
and you will be a mother, too
seem to casually be a part
of the familiar conversations
we uphold as a tradition
as if no other ambition
could ever be so satisfying
to help me finally realise
the rules that come
with being alive
today i reclaim my right
to feel actively offended
by those who dare imply
what womanhood means
in their language
as if a concept so wide and broad
could be restricted to a few words
as if a basic definition
or crazy expectations
should somewhat change
the eradicated perception
that dwells inside myself

                    i am   w e a r y
of seeing my future
narrowed down on the daily
i am   w e a r y
of the way my words
entangle on my tongue
when you find the nerve to demand
about the boyfriend i should have
at a table full of guests
who brought assumptions as a present
if only you could see your faces
as you proceed to claim
i am oh so pretty
it's almost a shame
that i am not yet in touch
with the one i'm longing for

                    must i say, if i'm allowed
                    the man of my dreams
                    you ramble about
                    appears much to be

the man of yours, instead

no evidence of witchcraft
will be found here on this land
no hunt or purge
nor burnt poor souls
will bite the dust
before our eyes

you mark sorcery
behind our back
and ignite a fire
in between our legs

wouldn't it be easier
to just accept
the power of our
charming spell?

how bold of you
to raise such a panic
when you could just accept
that we are made of magic

—- not witches
    but we can enchant you indeed

would you please just realise
how evil rivers lose their weight
as they press down
and down your spine
but fail to take your breath away

you're surrounded by all this blue
but would you just look at you
not a single drop you spilt
not a fish less in the sea

you can flourish
with no semen
and by all means
you are allowed
to seize those roses
and put them down
let them thrive
inside the vase
that you have shaped
with your own hands

because you
you are all the jars
you've put together
you are the circles

you have drawn
around the pole

you are all the miles you ran
and no other half is needed
for you to finally be a whole

you are not
a stairway to heaven
for others to step on
you are each one
of the countless times
you flooded pots with water

you are all the miles you ran
carrying steady on your head
the burden of a revolution

you are all the jars
you've put together
by drawing circles
around the pole
so no other half is needed
for you to finally be a whole

you long for a train
in the midst of the desert
but as you wait
you fail to embrace
the greatness of
how far you came

you are the fire
who brought lights
to dozens of roads
and thousands of lives

you'll teach your offspring
not to follow the footprint
of those who sowed hate
on the land we share

but what is it
that makes you so scared
of the same holy spring
in two pairs of legs?

your precious legacy
will forever stream
in the endless oceans
i'll give birth to

the sea will show me the way
to a greater universe
and on my way back
you'll be seeking water
on the shore of two rivers
who couldn't stop intertwining

— let my nature thrive

not much fairness
travels our way
to be considered
the fairer sex

—- women need answers
more than your companionship

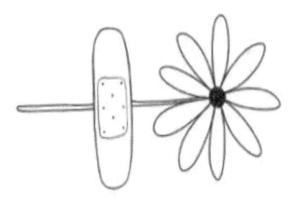

my beauty
is not defined
by a shoulder-length hairstyle
framing my face
as a perfect painting
watch me cut off
what weighs me down
and be a masterpiece
just as well

so next time
you trip over the strands
of the fur you wished i carried
i hope your eyes
will be free of the threads
that seem to keep you
from comprehending

what i did
i did for myself

i chopped off those fifteen inches
and on my head still lays a crown
i just let go of so much more
than you can wrap your head around

— miss me with the canonical expectations
you pin on women as avocation

you endured your pain
when no one else could have
and every hand they handed seemed so vain.
you rose your eyes from the pavement
when familiar fears led your attention
towards anything but your true self
yet you did face your reflection
with the fierceness of twenty beasts.
for every time you crawled
and stumbled on your feet,
you learnt how to walk again
and put to sleep all the complaints.
so now hush each of the birds
and don't shove your limbs into a rush
for you're so worthy of this rest.
can't you see you already won
against the echoes of your past?

— resilience bears so much power
it amazes me sometimes

one day
blooms will flourish
from me again
weeds will sew
my broken tissues
and mend them all
in a silent kiss

        wait for the time
        when failure will be buried
        and its flesh will find new light
        in the crisp wind of fresh success

    i will embrace
    one day
    blooms will flourish
    from me again
    weeds will sew

    my refound self
    and hug her tight
    and kiss her scars
    i will undress her
    'til she remembers
    that there is no
    shame in pleasure

at the sight of trees
that will have ripened
from my burnt ashes;
the heaviness of fruits
won't make them
slip back by the roots
for the sky is just too high
not to allow us
from time to time
to rise higher than
the beloved sun

— the road to healing is already here
and he's awaiting to be travelled across